SIGHT

Jill Bennett
and
Roger Smith

Macdonald Educational

How to use this book

First, look at the contents page opposite. Read the chapter list to see if it includes the subject you want. The list tells you what each page is about. You can then find the page with the information you need.

If you want to know about one particular thing, look it up in the index on page 31. For example, if you want to know about blinking, the index tells you that there is something about it on page 14. The index also lists the pictures in the book.

When you read this book, you will find some unusual words. The glossary on page 30 explains what they mean.

Series Editor
Margaret Conroy

Book Editor
Suzanne Greene

Production
Susan Mead

Picture Research
Kathy Lockley

Factual Adviser
David Edgar
Department of Optometry
& Visual Science, City University

Reading Consultant
Amy Gibbs
Inner London Education Authority
Centre for Language in Primary
Education

Series Design
Robert Mathias/Anne Isseyegh

Book Design
Julia Osorno/Anne Isseyegh

Teacher Panel
Sue Frolish, Diane Jackson,
Joanne Waterhouse

Illustrations
Dave Eaton Front cover
Bill le Fever/Linda Rogers Associates
Pages 8-9, 13, 22-23, 28-29
Tony Morris/Linda Rogers Associates
Pages 6-7, 10-11, 18-19, 24-25
Joanna Stubbs/B L Kearley Ltd
Pages 14-15, 16-17, 20-21

Photographs
Aldus Archive: cover photos
Heather Angel: 9, 12
Rex Features: 25
Suzanne Greene: 8, 14
Robert Harding: 15
RNIB/ILEA: 24
Science Photo Library: 16, 17

CONTENTS

EYES AND SEEING

Why we need eyes

This book is about sight and seeing. Sight is one of the five senses which we use to find out about the world around us. The other senses are hearing, taste, touch and smell. Many people think that sight is the most important of the five senses for humans. Do you agree? Imagine what it is like to eat, get dressed, play and go to school if you cannot see.

The way things look make us think and feel about them in certain ways. Bright colours usually make us feel more cheerful than dull or dark colours do. Your eyes are very powerful. They can see stars far away in space, and they can also see tiny details in flowers on the ground.

For many animals, other senses are more important than sight. Bats hunt for food at night, and so they cannot use their eyes to tell them where they are going. They make a squeaking noise which echoes off the objects all around. Bats' ears are so powerful that they can tell exactly where things are by listening to the way the echo bounces off them. Each kind of animal uses the senses which are most suited to the way it lives.

Moles live underground. It is always dark, and they have bad eyesight. A mole uses its snout, whiskers and hands to find its way.

6

The human brain uses all five senses to learn about the world. We use our eyes and ears most of the time that we are awake.

A rabbit's eyes and ears are at the sides of its head, so that it can see and hear all around. This helps it to escape from enemies.

A dog mainly uses its sensitive ears and nose, along with its eyes. Dogs can smell and hear many things which humans cannot.

What are eyes?

Your eyes are two round balls filled with jelly. The jelly, along with a watery liquid at the front of each eyeball, helps your eyes keep their ball-like shape. Each eye rests in a hollow in your skull.

The black dot in the middle of your eye is called the pupil. It is really a hole that lets light into your eye. The coloured ring around your pupil is called the iris. In front of the iris and the pupil is a colourless, curved surface called the cornea. It is transparent and lets the light come through. Behind your pupil is the lens. It is clear, soft and flexible. What you call the white of your eye is the sclera. This protects the whole eye, except the cornea.

At the back of your eye is the retina. The optic nerve connects your eye to your brain. It leads from the retina to the brain.

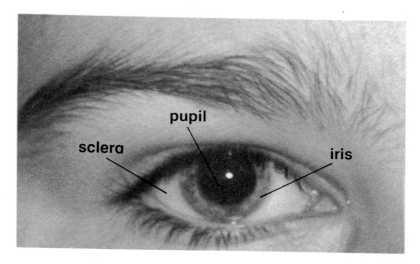

An eye as we see it from in front.

An insect's eyes are made up of many very simple eyes, and are called compound eyes. Compound eyes don't see as clearly as human eyes.

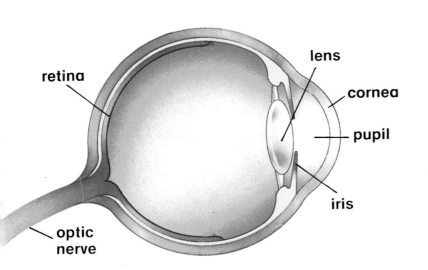

This is what an eye would look like if we could see into it from the side.

9

How do we see?

Light is made up of many rays, which all travel in a straight line. When they hit an object, they bounce off it. All objects have light rays bouncing off them, except when it is dark. If you are looking at an object, the light rays go into your eyes.

When light enters your eye, the cornea and the lens bend the rays inwards, so that they make an image on the retina, which is like a screen at the back of your eye.

The retina has two types of cell, called rods and cones. They send tiny electrical signals to the brain, telling it about the brightness and colour of what you are looking at. Rods help you to see shades of grey, and cones help you to see colour and fine detail.

The signals from the rods and cones travel along the optic nerve, which leads from the eye to the brain. Your brain can now make a picture, and you see what you are looking at.

You can choose what you look at by moving your eyes in almost any direction. Six muscles move each eye up, down, right, left, or around. Both of your eyes should be looking in the same direction at the same time.

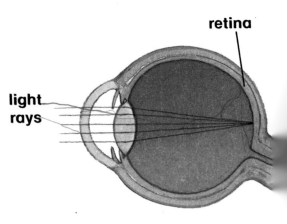

light rays

retina

Light rays enter your eye through the cornea and pupil. The rays are bent so that they fall on to the retina at the back of the eye.

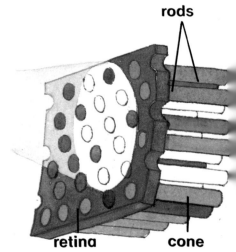

rods

retina   cone

In dim light rods turn from purple to white, and enable us to see. Cones change to white only when bright light hits them.

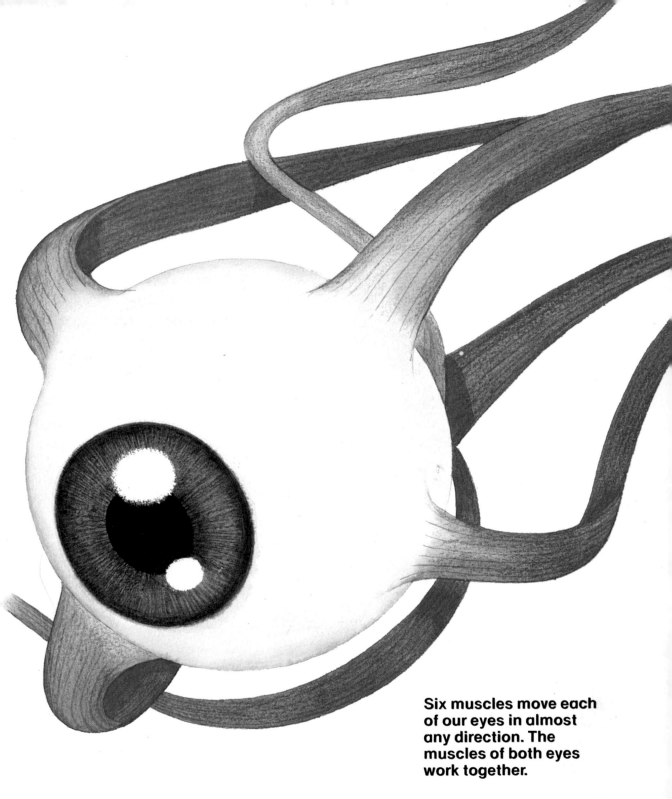

Six muscles move each
of our eyes in almost
any direction. The
muscles of both eyes
work together.

Focusing

When light rays form an image of an object on your retina, the image has to be clear for you to see the object properly. If you can see an object clearly, we say that it is in focus and if you do not see it clearly, we say that it is out of focus.

If you look around you, it probably seems as though you can see everything clearly, but this is not really true. Your eyes have to focus in one way for an object which is nearby, and in another way for an object which is far away. You cannot focus in both ways at the same time.

A chameleon can move each eye separately. It can focus on something behind and something in front of it at the same time. This helps it to spot enemies easily.

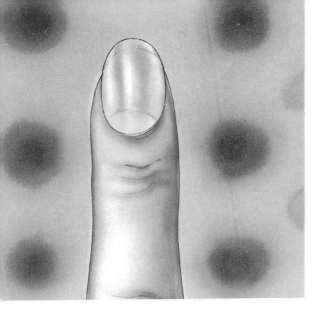
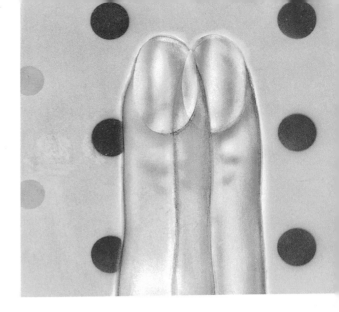

If you look at your finger so that it is in focus, the background behind it will be out of focus. It will look blurred, as it is in the picture.

If you look beyond your finger, so that the background is in focus, your finger will be out of focus, and you may see a double image of it.

The lens in your eye changes shape quickly and easily. As it does this it changes the way the light rays bend. This helps you to see in focus.

When you look at something nearby, the lens becomes rounder and the light rays bend inward more. When you look at something far away, your lens gets flatter, and the light rays bend inward less sharply.

Your lens is changing shape all the time, as you look at things at different distances from you. You do not notice that your lens is changing because it happens so quickly and easily.

13

Protecting our eyes

Your eyes are delicate and they need to be protected. Eyes are set back in your head. Your forehead, which is bony and hard, sticks out a little over the eyes, and your cheekbones stick out a little under your eyes. This gives good, natural protection to your eyes.

Your eyebrows and eyelashes are there to protect your eyes, too. If rain or sweat is rolling down your forehead, the eyebrows stop it from going into your eyes, and eyelashes act as traps to catch dirt and dust before they can get into your eye.

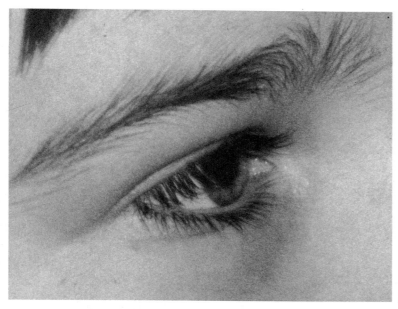

Your eyebrows, eyelashes, eyelids and tears all give natural protection to your eyes.

Sometimes we use extra protection for our eyes. Count the different ways these children shield their eyes from the Sun and sea.

14

Your eyelids are moved by muscles. You've probably noticed that your eyes close very quickly if you look at a bright light, or that you blink if something is coming too close to your eye. Blinking is a way of protecting your eyes.

Blinking spreads tears over your eyeball. Tears help protect your eyes by washing any dirt or dust to the bottom of your eye. Then the tears drain away through the tear duct, into the nose. If you tasted your tears, you would find that they are salty. Salt helps to kill germs.

This metal-worker wears special glasses to stop his eyes being hurt by bright, hot sparks.

15

EYE AND BRAIN

Pupil and retina

When the light is bright, the iris, which is the coloured part of your eye, gets wider. This makes your pupil smaller, so that less light enters the eye. When the light is dim, your iris gets narrower, so your pupil gets bigger, and more light can enter your eye. In this way, your eyes make sure that the right amount of light gets into them.

When light rays enter an eye, they cross over before they reach the retina. This means that light rays coming from the top of an object will hit the bottom of your retina, and light rays coming from the bottom of the object will hit the top. So the image of what you are looking at is upside down on your retina.

The rods and cones in your retina send messages along the optic nerve to your brain, telling it what the image looks like. Your brain makes a picture from what the messages tell it. Although the image on your retina is upside down, your brain knows which way up the picture should be. It turns the picture the right way up, and so what you see makes sense in the world that you know.

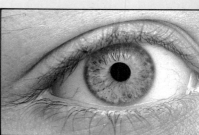

In bright light, your iris gets wider and your pupil becomes smaller. Less light enters your eye.

16

Thanks to his badge of courage, Simon made more and more friends.

Everyone wanted to share how they were different too.

**Simon's favorite new friend
was Coco**, a small robin who loved
to tell stories and teach.

"Looking at your beak makes me smile,"
said Coco. "I have so much fun laughing and chirping
with you that I don't even notice your beak."

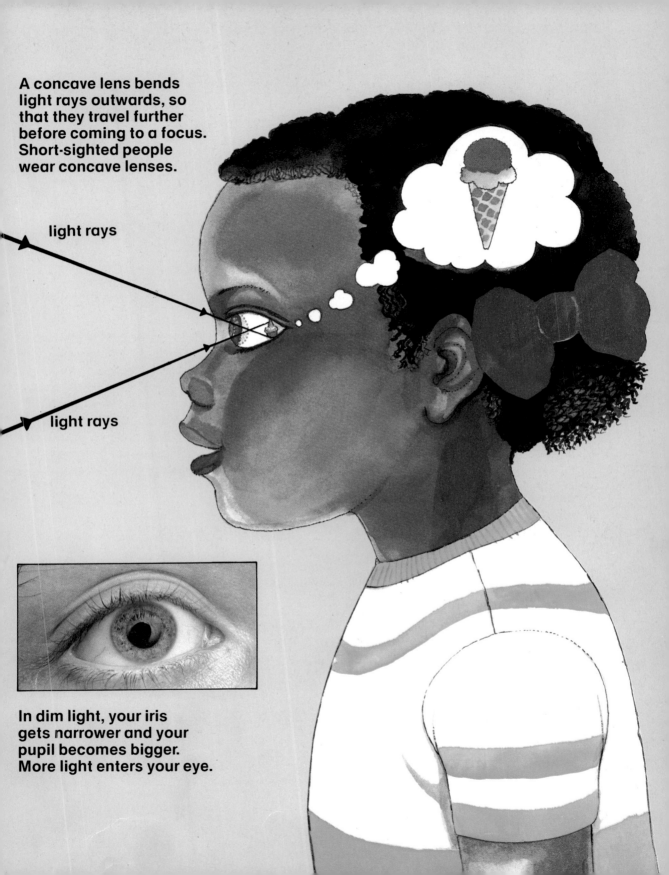

A concave lens bends light rays outwards, so that they travel further before coming to a focus. Short-sighted people wear concave lenses.

light rays

light rays

In dim light, your iris gets narrower and your pupil becomes bigger. More light enters your eye.

Binocular vision

Rabbits and chickens have eyes at the sides of their heads. Each eye points in a different direction, and so they see two pictures at the same time. The eyes of human beings point in the same direction — forwards. Your eyes are about 5.5 centimetres apart, so each eye sees a slightly different picture. You do not realize this because your brain combines the two pictures into one. This type of vision is called stereoscopic or binocular vision.

Binocular vision means that we see things in three dimensions or '3-D', instead of flat like the pictures in this book. Seeing in '3-D' means that we can judge depth and distances.

Put one hand up above your head. Bring one finger down on to the tip of a pencil. Now try to do it with one eye closed. It's much more difficult. This is because you need both eyes for judging depth and distances.

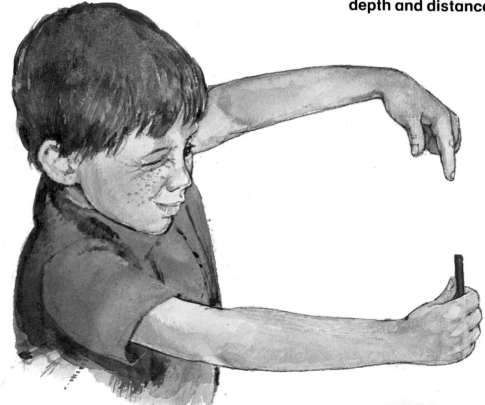

Humans, monkeys and apes can see about two-thirds of the way around them. Half of this is seen with both eyes, and the rest with only one eye. Using both eyes together makes it easier to judge depth and distance. This is important for the monkeys and apes that swing from tree to tree.

A rabbit can see all around itself. Only small areas in front and behind are seen with both eyes. Rabbits need to see all around because there are many animals which hunt them.

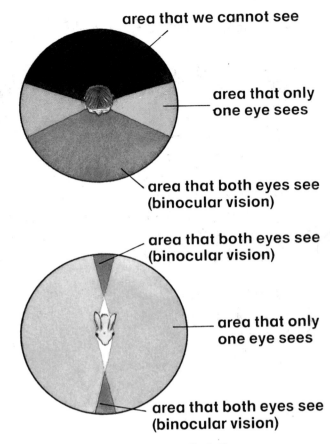

area that we cannot see

area that only one eye sees

area that both eyes see (binocular vision)

area that both eyes see (binocular vision)

area that only one eye sees

area that both eyes see (binocular vision)

You can see how each eye sees a slightly different picture by holding a pencil in front of you. Close your right eye, and look at the pencil with your left eye. Now close your left eye and look at the pencil with your right eye. The pencil seems to move slightly against the background, doesn't it?

If you only look through one eye, you do not see in '3-D', and it is hard to judge depth and distances. You can see what happens if you try the test on page 18.

Seeing colours

Mammals and most birds are the only creatures who are able to see in colour. Human eyes are very good at seeing colours.

You have almost 7 million cones in each retina. Cones are sensitive to coloured light, and they enable you to see colours and fine detail. You also have about 120 million rods in each retina. These rods are sensitive to the amount of light entering your eye and they enable you to see black, and shades of grey.

The colours of the rainbow are red, orange, yellow, green, blue, indigo and violet. All the colours we see are made up of one or more colours of the rainbow.

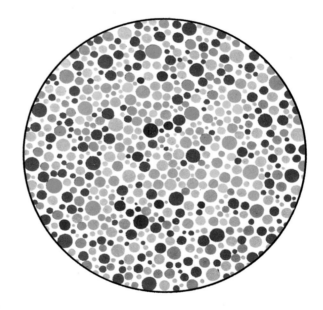

Tests for defective colour vision sometimes look like this. A person with full colour vision should be able to see the number in the circle. The number in this circle is 74.

One day, while Simon and Coco were talking,
something magical happened.
Simon's baby-brown feathers started to change color.

First, the soft downy feathers close to his skin
turned pink. Then, the feathers on his wings
changed to a bright, **beautiful red.**

"Look," Simon said.
"My feathers are smiling!"

"Yes," chirped Coco.
"They're very beautiful."

Simon was so excited by his feathers that he had to fly.

He flapped his wings and zoomed into the sky.

He zipped from tree to tree, smiling and calling
for all the birds to join him.

"Come fly! Come fly!" he sang.
"We are different, but we are beautiful!
We have a voice, so let's sing."

**"Let's spread our
wings** and seize the day,
remembering to be kind
along the way."

Soon, all the birds were coloring the sky with their beautiful
songs and smiles. They got so loud, that Patty and her mom
came out of the house to see what was happening.

Rods are more sensitive than cones, so when there is not much light, we only see in black, and shades of grey.

Sometimes people cannot see colours properly. We say that these people have defective colour vision.

Some people with defective colour vision cannot tell the difference between red and green, or between orange and yellow. About eight out of every hundred males have defective colour vision, but it is much more unusual in females.

The colours in this picture are those that people with full colour vision would see.

Some people with defective colour vision may see something like this when they look at the same picture.

SIGHT PROBLEMS

Long and short sight

If your eye is not a perfect ball shape, it may sometimes be difficult for you to focus properly. If your eyeball is too long from the lens to the retina, light rays would come to a focus before reaching your retina. So what you see is out of focus. This type of problem is called short sight.

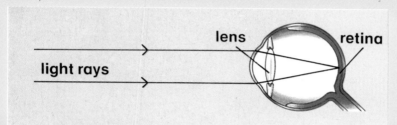

This eye has normal sight. Light rays come to a focus on the retina.

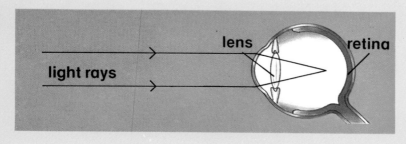

This eye has short sight. The light rays come to a focus before they reach the retina. When the light rays reach the retina, they are out of focus.

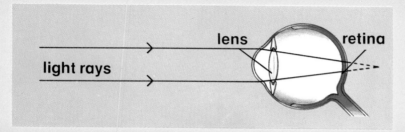

This eye has long sight. The light rays only come to a focus behind the retina. When the light rays reach the retina, they are not in focus.

"Look! Simon's feathers turned red," said Patty.

"Yes, and he has some new friends too," said Patty's mom.

"What a wonderful way to celebrate his badge of courage."

Smile with Simon
and be kind!

SMILE WITH SIMON

We may not be the same
and if we were it'd be a shame
you have a voice let go and sing
open up just spread your wings
you've got to feel good about yourself
you've got to feel good about yourself

I am different but I am beautiful
we are different but we are beautiful
we're still alike in many ways
cardinals, sparrows and blue jays
we fall sometimes but that's okay
pick yourself up and seize the day

so smile with Simon and be kind
smile and see what you will find
so smile with Simon this is his song
his badge of courage makes him strong

we are different but we are beautiful
Simon can lift you up my friend
so come fly and watch as we ascend
true friends are out there you will see
lean on them in times of need

so smile with Simon and be kind
smile and see what you will find
so smile with Simon this is his song
his badge of courage makes him strong

SIMON'S FAVORITES

AboutFace.ca
ACPA American Cleft Palate-Craniofacial Association
Bear Necessities Pediatric Cancer Foundation
Beauty with a Twist
BORN A HERO, Pfeiffer's Health and Social Issues Awareness
Camp About Face
Cary Kanno-Musical Artist
Children's Craniofacial Association (CCA Kids)
CleftProud
Cuddles For Clefts
Doctors Without Borders
Emory Cleft Project-Dept Human Genetics, Emory Univ School of Medicine
Face the Future Foundation Illinois
FACES: The National Craniofacial Association
Facing Forward Inc
Love Me Love My Face: Jono Lancaster
MyFace
National Organization for Rare Disorders (NORD)
Noordhoff Craniofacial Foundation Philippines, Inc
Operation of Hope Worldwide
Operation Smile
Patients Rising
Pete's Diary: Peter Dankelson. Motivational Speaker
Rare Disease Legislative Advocates (RDLA)
Joe Rutland -CleftThoughts
Smile Train
Solidarity Bridge.org
St. Jude Children's Research Hospital
UI Health Craniofacial Center at the UIC College of Medicine

ABOUT PATRICIA ANN SIMON

I am a RN and was born with a cleft lip and palate.

I have written four books, *Smile with Simon, Simon and the Buddy Branch, Simon and Patty Go To Camp,* and *Simon and the Bully.* These children's books resonate with young people suffering from similar craniofacial differences.

My first children's book, *Smile with Simon* is about a cardinal named Simon, who's born with a gap in his beak. His gap made it difficult for him to eat, smile, and sing. In the story, he meets a young girl named Patty, who relates with Simon because she has a cleft lip.

I wrote a second book, *Simon and the Buddy Branch,* which further stresses the importance of kindness, love, and acceptance in the lives of children with facial differences.

My aim is to help children born with facial differences understand that it's okay to be different. I want to remind them that they are beautiful.

I am also a member of American Cleft Palate-Craniofacial Association (ACPA), Children's Craniofacial Association (CCA), Cleft Community Advisory Council (CCAC) for Smile Train, and former board member of Face the Future Foundation, which supports the efforts of University of Illinois Health Craniofacial Center.

I have given a keynote speech for the Inaugural Cleft Lip and Palate Team Day at Morgan Stanley Children's Hospital in New York Presbyterian Hospital,

My book, *Smile with Simon* was translated to Tagalog so that it could be used at a Philippine speech camp.

I created a webpage, www.smilewithsimon.org which features videos and songs that reinforce the message we are all different, and to be accepting and kind.

Books can be purchased directly through my website:
www.smilewithsimon.org

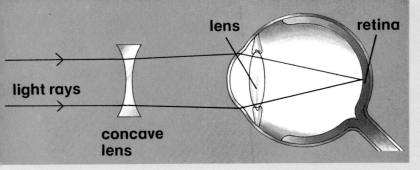

light rays

concave
lens

lens   retina

A concave lens bends
light rays outwards, so
that they travel further
before coming to a focus.
Short-sighted people
wear concave lenses to
help them see in focus.

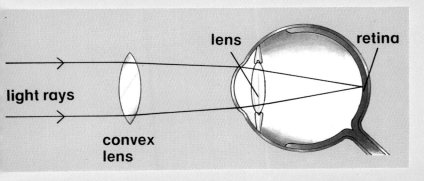

light rays

convex
lens

lens   retina

A convex lens bends
light rays inwards, so
that they come to a
focus at an earlier point.
Long-sighted people
wear convex lenses to
help them see in focus.

If your eyeball is too short from the lens
to the retina, light rays would come to a
focus beyond the retina. So what you see is
out of focus. This type of problem is called
long sight.

Short-sighted people usually wear glasses
to help them focus on distant objects.
These glasses have lenses which bend light
rays outwards before they enter the eye, so
that they come to a focus on the retina.
The shape of the lenses is called concave.

Long-sighted people sometimes wear glasses
for focusing on nearby objects. The glasses
have lenses which bend light rays inward
before they enter the eye, so that they
come to a focus on the retina. The shape of
these lenses is called convex.

Being blind

It is very hard to imagine what it is like
to be blind. Close your eyes and cover them
with your hands. It's very dark, isn't it?
Can you see anything? Blind people cannot
see anything, even in very bright light with
their eyes open. Some people are blind
when they are born. Others go blind later,
because of an illness or an accident.

Blind people use the other senses to find out
about the world around them. They can learn
to live their lives without sight.

**This blind boy is
learning to shoot at a
target with a bow and
arrow. Blind people play
many different sports.**

Stevie Wonder is a famous singer and musician. He is one of many blind people who have very successful careers.

Blind people cannot read books with their eyes, so they learn to read special books. In these books letters and numbers are made from tiny bumps which stick up from the page. These bumps make patterns which blind people can feel with their fingertips. This system is called Braille.

When blind people go out they may use a stick to help them feel where they are going. Some blind people have guide-dogs which are trained to act as their eyes.

FINDING OUT MORE

Experiments

Most of us have one eye which is stronger than the other one. We call this eye the dominant eye. You can find out which it is. Hold your hands together and point your index fingers at the corner of an object. Look at the object with both eyes open. Now close your left eye and look at it with your right eye. Now close your right eye and look at the object with your left eye. The fingers probably seem to jump to one side when a particular eye is open. This means that the eye which is closed is the dominant eye.

Sometimes your brain thinks it sees things which are not there. Your eyes can confuse your own brain! Hold your index fingers together about 5 centimetres in front of your eyes. Now stare beyond your fingers. You will see a small sausage shape between your fingers, but you know that it is not really there!

There are no rods and cones on the part of the eye where the optic nerve leaves it. This means that no signals go to your brain, and so you cannot see anything on this part of the eye. This gives you a 'blind spot'.

●

Find your blind spot. Hold this book about 15 centimetres in front of your eyes. Close your left eye and stare at the red dot with your right eye, moving the book slowly towards you and then away from you. When the red cross disappears from sight, the cross is hitting your blind spot. To find the blind spot in your left eye, do the test staring at the cross, with your right eye shut.

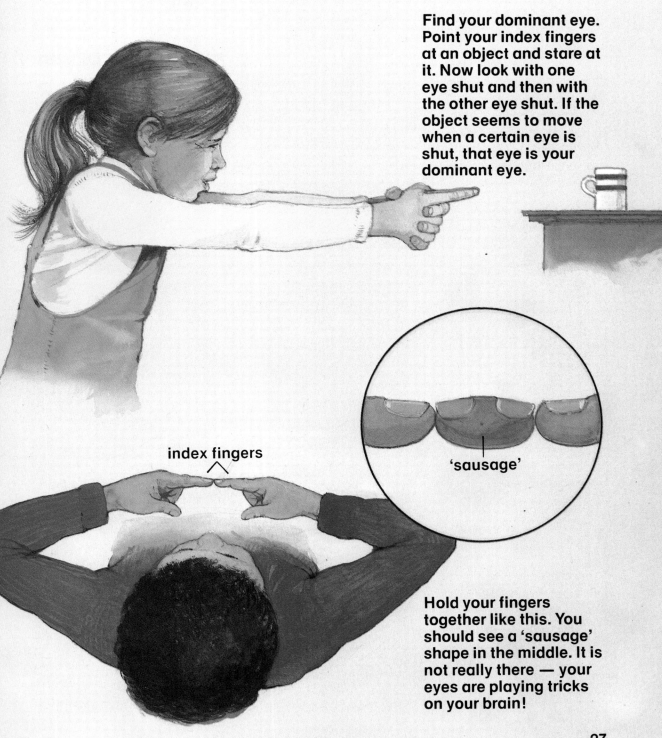

Find your dominant eye. Point your index fingers at an object and stare at it. Now look with one eye shut and then with the other eye shut. If the object seems to move when a certain eye is shut, that eye is your dominant eye.

index fingers

'sausage'

Hold your fingers together like this. You should see a 'sausage' shape in the middle. It is not really there — your eyes are playing tricks on your brain!

Optical illusions

Which line looks longer? They are both the same length, but your brain thinks that the bottom one is longer. This is an optical illusion.

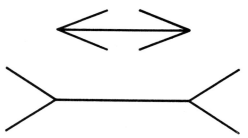

Sometimes, things are not quite what they seem to be. Your brain tries to make sense of all the images that the eye sends it. If your eyes see something that your brain cannot understand, your brain likes to change the picture, so that it fits in with what you already know.

This is why you sometimes think you see things that are not really there. This type of trick played by your eyes on your brain is called an optical illusion.

Your brain always tries to make sense of what it sees. If you stare at this picture it will sometimes look like a white vase, and sometimes like two purple faces.

Sometimes your brain is tricked because you look at an object from a different angle or in a different light from the one in which you usually view it.

People can use optical illusions to make us think about things in a certain way. If a company is trying to sell a product, it may photograph it using an angle and lighting which make the product seem bigger and better. This may make more people buy it.

Scientists have been studying optical illusions for hundreds of years. They do not yet agree on how and why all of them work.

This optical illusion makes your brain think that the two thick lines are curved. If you hold a ruler against them, you will find that they are straight lines.

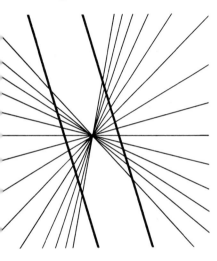

Your brain always puts things in order. If you stare at this picture, you will see several different patterns on it.

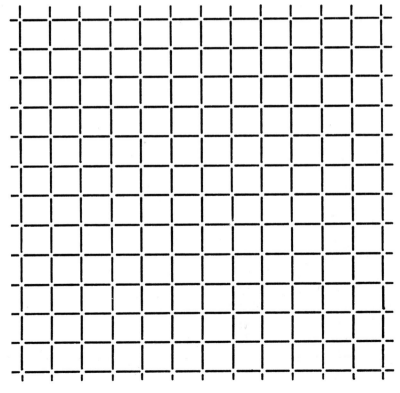

29

GLOSSARY, BOOKS TO READ

A glossary is a word list. This one explains unusual words that are used in this book.

Binocular vision Seeing almost the same picture at once with two eyes. Humans, monkeys and apes have binocular vision, and this helps them to judge depth and distance.

Braille A special kind of printing in books, in which letters and numbers are made of dots and bumps which stick up from the page. Blind people read Braille with their fingertips.

Cell A tiny part of your body. Your whole body is made of millions and millions of tiny cells.

Concave lens A lens which is thicker at the edges than in the middle. It bends light rays outwards and is used to correct short sight.

Cones Cells in the retina which enable you to see colours and fine detail.

Convex lens A lens which is thicker in the middle than at the sides. It bends light rays inwards, and is used to correct long sight.

Focusing Bending light rays so that they form a clear image, on your retina, for example.

Image The image of an object is made when light rays bounce off the object and form a picture of it on your retina.

Iris The coloured ring surrounding your pupil. It controls the amount of light entering the pupil. As the iris gets wider, your pupil becomes smaller, and as the iris gets narrower, your pupil becomes bigger.

Lens The transparent part of the eye behind the pupil. It focuses light on to the retina.

Light rays Light is made up of many light rays. They always travel in straight lines.

Optic nerve A bundle of nerves which carry messages from each eye to the brain.

Retina The screen at the back of your eye. This is where light rays are focused to produce an image.

Rods Cells in the retina which enable you to see in black, and shades of grey.

Senses The five ways in which humans find out about the world around them. The five different senses are: sight, hearing, touch, taste and smell.

BOOKS TO READ

Body Facts by Alan Maryon-Davis, Macdonald 1984.
It is harder to read than this book, but it's fun, and has very good pictures.

Me and You (My First Encyclopedia, volume 1) by Joanna Howard, Macdonald Educational 1982.

Sally Can't See by Palle Peterson, A&C Black 1976.

Sight by Ed Catherall, Wayland, 1981.
This book is full of tests and experiments for you to try.

The Eye and Seeing by Brian R. Ward, Franklin Watts, 1981.
This explains sight in more detail, and it is a bit harder to read, but it has lots of pictures.

Your Senses by Dorothy Baldwin and Claire Lister, Wayland, 1983.